PUSHed

(Pray Until Something Happens *Everyday*)

DEONTE MOSS

Pushed

PUSHed (Pray Until Something Happens Everyday)
ISBN: 978-0-578-55142-5

Book Cover by: Info@innomarkgroup.com

Formatting by: Pieces of Me Publications, LLC
Number: 419-322-0438
Email: pom@piecesofmepublications.com
Website: www.piecesofmepublications.com

Table of Contents

Introduction

It took me forever to write this book.

The crazy part is I knew I had to do it and heard God clearly and still procrastinated.

He told when I wrote the book, he would put me in the position I wanted to be in.

After I was done doing what he told me to do. I originally was going to name the book "PUSH" based on the acronym pray until something happens.

But after a series of events and God sharpening me, he told me a few years ago to name the book "PUSHED" (Pray Until Something Happens Every Day)

And it wasn't until I really built the appropriate relationship with God, that I needed that he allowed me to release the book.

We need God every day, not just when we feel we need him or when things are going bad in our lives.

God has taught me this lesson and he did it with prayer.

I believe prayer is a mindset.

When I tell you I pray all day every day, don't just think I am closing my eyes and kneeling all day.

Although there are times I do find time to close my eyes or kneel and talk to God.

Prayer is so much more than that. Prayer could be singing a song, worshipping God, standing or sitting in complete silence in your home or car.

It could be quoting or writing scriptures, even reading your word or spiritual books, watching a spiritual or educational TV show, movie or the YouTube channel.

Plus, it doesn't always have to be done alone. It can be done with one, two, three or many people, and not even necessarily in the same place.

Just know when praying, faith without works is dead. (James 2:17).

So there will always be an action to compliment your prayer to receive what you're asking God for.

So when I say I pray all day everyday just know I am singing, quoting, meditating, thinking, watching, writing and teaching with GOD on my mind.

Don't forget to pray; don't be ashamed to pray and don't be too proud to pray because prayer changes things.

This is my story and how I overcame the challenges of a being a high-risk black boy battling alcohol and drug addicted parents, severe behaviors in school, and countless encounters with the juvenile justice system and multiple experiences navigating the foster care system.

Prayer saved me.

Today, I am a man of God who loves being a husband, father, teacher, entrepreneur and author.

I believe I was God sent to save my family like Joseph in Bible, but also like Moses to a generation. Let my people go …

<u>*Chapter 1*</u>

The
Struggle
Couldn't Stop Me

I always wanted to tell my story, but had no clue where to start.

Then one day, God told me to start from the beginning.

My name is Deonte Moss, and I was born July 18, 1985, to a mother who was addicted to crack cocaine, and a father who sold drugs.

My mother smoked crack cocaine throughout her entire pregnancy with me.

My parents had three children, in which I was the oldest.

I don't have many memories of my toddler years, just a few vague memories here and there.

Most of the memories I can easily recall involve my life with grandmother, who I refer to as Nana, and her mother, my great-grandmother, who I refer to as Mother.

I can also easily recall many of my experiences living in 10 different foster homes and four group homes.

The struggle, the experiences and the calling on my life, I know God prepared me for this day through it all.

It took me five years to graduate high school.

And when I did graduate, I had a 0.7 grade point average.

That's right. I bet you didn't even think that was possible.

Ha! Anything is possible.

I'll never forget it because the valedictorian of my class had a 4.7 GPA, and I was like whoa, he got a whole 4.0 GPA more than me.

This is one of the many reasons I constantly speak with children about the importance of getting their GPA high during their early years of high school.

I often tell them this provides them with a little cushion in the latter years.

Unfortunate for me, I did things backwards. I did horrible early on, and then tried to raise my GPA in my later years of high school.

I ended up having to add an additional year to my high school career, so I know from experience.

I was a class clown my first three years of high school. I received mostly zeros and F's.

When my upperclassmen years were approaching, I had a lot of work to do.

I was trying to fix my grades to graduate. I had to transfer to a different school because their credit system was more beneficial for me then my public school I was attending. I was able to earn credits a lot quicker.

I quickly realized there was an enormous difference between public inner-city schools and the suburban school I attended.

My public school work was done together, and my grade was almost based on behavior and participation.

My suburban experience really challenged me and prepared me for college. I graduated in two and half years. I repeat, the valedictorian held a 4.7 GPA. I had a .7 GPA. I was at the bottom of my class.

I then went to college off a scholarship.

How's that you ask?

Well, you know it wasn't academic.

It was an orphan scholarship for emancipating or growing up in foster care as a youth.

We called them ETV funds. The only college that would accept me was the University of Toledo and that was only because it had open enrollment.

I did well my first year.

It wasn't that I had what seemed like starter up college courses, although I might not have gotten all what was being taught. I participated and showed up every day.

Initially, I studied pre-med to become a pediatrician thinking more bang for my buck. But that quickly changed.

Then I switched to broadcasting and communication with a minor in theatre. I ended my first semester out with a 3.7 GPA, and then partying began.

I ended up on academic probation and lost my scholarship that following year. Eventually, I lost my housing and ended up on my best friend's living room floor for a while before being able to afford an apartment.

Later, I tried to go to a school online, but never took it seriously. I only applied for the refund check to buy a car, which eventually was repossessed.

After initially flunking out of college, higher education was put on the back burner and I started working full time. I began my careers of working inside schools.

I started working with students as a behavior coach. I really enjoyed this role. And this time away from school, ignited another passion of mine.

After some soul searching, I eventually decided to go to school to learn more about religion and my favorite book. I studied biblical studies and eventually received my associate degree, then bachelor's, followed by my master's degree.

<u>Chapter 2</u>

My
Earliest
Memories

When I was three, I recall my father going to prison. I don't remember much from that age, but I'm reminded by my mother from stories she tells me.

She tells us stories of how it was before she left my sisters and me. My mother would tell me stories about her life. She would tell me about how hard it was to deal with my father.

My mother told me all about the abuse she had to endure, as well as some of the good times her and my father had together. She referred to my father as the ladies' man. She would tell me stories about all the women he had, and how he would try to shyster his way back into her life every time she prepared to leave him.

There are two stories in particular that I always remember.

My father, according to my mother, was abusive at times.

One time after my father had beat my mom, he would never want her to leave.

My mother would always plan to leave so he would do things to convince her to stay.

There was one time where he threatened to kill himself.

He grabbed his gun, locked himself in a bedroom and pulled the trigger.

My mother was trying her hardest to get into the bedroom. She could not get in the room, so she called the police.

When the police arrived, they broke down the door and realized my father had jumped out the window. To my mother's surprise, my father had fired a random shot to mislead my mother and make her think he killed himself.

On another occasion when my mother threatened to leave my father after he beat her, my father, who was lactose intolerant, decided to elude my mother again.

My father drank milk and poured bleach on the floor. He then laid in the bleach and spit the milk out of his mouth causing it to appear as foam.

As my mother was preparing to leave, she found my father in the kitchen foaming from the mouth. She quickly ran to call the police. As my mother was calling for help, my father jumped up to tell her he was fine and had only baffled her in hopes of getting her to stay.

I do remember being with my biological parents, but only a few things like my first whipping.

I don't think anyone forgets there first whipping. It was a group whipping to. I and the neighbor's kids and cousins got it for tearing up a bedroom while the parents were downstairs partying.

I remember my first dog. My father introduced us to the pet and I was so excited, and so was he.

The puppy chased me and I took off thinking he was attacking me.

I fell. He licked my face and I burst out crying. I remember my Nana buying me a batman big wheel and life size Alf stuffed animal for Christmas. I remember my first power wheeled jeep. There are a lot of things I do not remember, but it crazy to me how the mind picks up things you seen before that are hidden deep down inside of us.

<u>*Chapter 3*</u>

Thank
God
For Nana

So when I was three, my father left for prison.

I assume my mother felt nothing was holding her back. I'm not sure if it was my father or the addiction, but she took us to my Nana's, my father's mother's house, my grandmother, and never returned, leaving my two younger sister and me.

I recall days of waiting for my mom to come to pick us up, but those days never came.

Life wasn't so bad with my Nana. She was very successful. She had a master's degree, was a certified social worker and was a mental health counselor. However, I think it was hard for her to care for three young children because she was much older.

I lived with my Nana until I was about 8 years old. Within those five years, what I remember most was from my Nana was that God loved me. My Nana taught me that.

She had us involved in everything. I took gymnastics, drum lessons and karate. I thank God for my Nana because not only did she take the responsibility of raising us, she was ironing out the issues of her own children while trusting God.

My grandmother had six children: four sons and two daughters. One of my aunts died as baby.

My oldest uncle on my dad's side of the family is a very successful journalist.

My fondest memory of him was dancing at his wedding all night long and all the family and friends cheering me on.

Under him was another uncle, who I remember fun times with and living with him for a summer with my cousins.

He had three children: two sons and a daughter; and he adopted a nephew. He has since passed away. He was only 39.

I have another uncle who has dreams of being a musician, but has serious health complications in his legs.

This is probably the uncle I spent the most time with in my early years due to him babysitting me and my sister when my Nana was working.

He never drove and would walk us all around town to meet up with girls or his crazy drunk friends.

Two memories that stick out the most with my uncle was one whipping he gave me inside a door way of my Nana's house.

I could not wait to get older just to let him know that I remember that whipping.

Another time was when I received my first Charlie horse in my leg and my uncle made a pot of warm water to put my foot in to submerge the pain I was in.

For my only living aunt, I remember she was on drugs very bad. She had told me once that her drug problem started when she felt my Nana made her get an abortion at an early age.

My father who is the youngest, loves his mother to death. I just recently found out that my father did not have the same father as his brothers and sister.

As long as I could remember, I've never known someone as strong as my Nana who loved God with her whole life.

I mean we were heavily involved in church picnics, programs and fundraisers. My Nana has kept my sisters involved in many things such as ballet, dance and even Girls Scouts.

I remember one time we went to an amusement park with the Girl Scouts when I was about 6 with my sisters and I got lost for hours. I was picked up by two younger women who called me their boyfriend and did not turn me in until later that night when security finally called my Nana to say they found me. My Nana was a proud sorority member. She kept us in the best schools. I was in Catholic schools until I was taken away from her. My Nana still until this day warms my heart with joy whenever I talk to her.

She has had some heart issues that has kept her in and out the hospital the past few years.

But she has bounced back greatly, all while still taking care of another grandson and my aunt and her husband, who I ironically call uncle.

Chapter 4

My First Experience In Foster Care

I was taken away from my Nana under an investigation from children services (CSB.) I was separated from my sisters and placed in a foster home.

I was hurt because I didn't want to be separated from the only family that I had; my sisters. They went to a separate foster home together and I was sent to a separate home alone.

My first foster family was with a very old couple. I spent that entire summer with them, but barely, rarely ever spoke to them. I just did not want to be there.

I would lock myself in the room with no television, just a clock radio in which only one station worked, which wasn't even my preference of music, but I quickly learned all the songs.

I remember it like it was yesterday. ("I'm a Barbie girl in a Barbie world...)(Ummm Bop du do do wop...).

Children Services knew that I wasn't speaking and eventually decided to put me in another foster home with more children so that I would interact.

They ended up putting me into a foster home with a group of boys. We lived with this woman we called, Big Momma.

I loved Big Momma's house. She was nice, and the boys who lived there were cool, also. We played sports with each other and had a real family setting.

Big Momma was my first real mother figure I could remember, and I was nine years old. I stayed with Big Momma for about two years.

The only reason why I left was because she had passed away. Big Momma's death was bitter sweet for me. At this time, I had found out my birth mother was getting clean.

She was doing what she needed to do to get my sisters and me out of foster care. It was a happy moment for me because I didn't desire to be a foster kid, and I wanted to get to know my birth mother. I wanted to get to know my real mom, plus I would be reunited with my sisters.

Now, I lived in 10 foster homes four group homes. Most of my foster homes were temporary placement before I reached a permanent home.

I barely remember even most of them. My most influential foster home was the home of my spiritual father, who raised and mentored me from about 12 years old.

He originally was a substitute teacher of mine and he started mentoring me and taking me to church with him when I was about 14 years old. I had never seen a man love or trust God the way he did, and it impacted me seriously.

I wanted that relationship he had with God for myself. I eventually would move in with him and when my mother went to prison, he filed for his foster care license to keep me.

Chapter 5

Me Vs. Him

Pushed

My mom was awarded custody of my sister and me, and we moved back with her. Things were looking good!

My mom had introduced us to her boyfriend and we were going to create the family that we always wanted.

Everything was great for about six months. One day, my mom's boyfriend lost his temper and slammed me for washing dishes.

My mom didn't know what to do. She came to my aide, but he pushed her away, and things started to fall apart after that. My mom's boyfriend was 25 years older than her. He was slim man with long wavy hair.

Eventually, my mother's boyfriend started hitting on her, and he picked up a bad addiction to crack cocaine. I remember one day catching him smoke through a crack in his bedroom door.

Not long after that, I realized he had an addiction. I was wise enough to realize he also was a pimp.

My mom's boyfriend became her pimp and started prostituting my mom. He would set up shop right in the comforts of our own home. Johns would knock on the doors and some even rented a downstairs bedroom and would stay for extended periods of time.

26

I quietly grew to have strong negative feelings toward my mother's boyfriend. I could not stand him and remember thinking of the things I wanted to do to him to protect my family.

At around age 10, I noticed my sister would spend a lot of time in mother's room with her boyfriend. She would began getting extra attention and small gifts.

I knew something wasn't right, but I couldn't quite put my finger on it immediately. However, it didn't take long for me to realize he was molesting my sister.

I do remember him getting into an argument with my mom about him wanting to bathe my sisters telling her he missed out on his daughters growing up and wanted to relive those moments with my sisters.

And as I got older, I realized in every picture my sister was attached to him, either sitting in his lap or holding his hand. He would rape my sister and force her to do drugs with him.

Eventually, my mother's boyfriend introduced my sister to prostituting too. My mom and my sister started working together. My little sister was no older than 12 years old when she began prostituting.

I do not remember the exact day when my sister started prostituting and using drugs, but I do remember her being in my mom's boyfriend's room for extended periods of time.

I even remember her getting into a fist fight with my mom about my mom accusing her of stealing her boyfriend. At this point in my life, our home became crazy.

My mom and her boyfriend pimp would argue, and fight and my mom would disappear for weeks at a time with no trace or site of her. The whole time, it seemed my sister had replaced her in the absence of my mother.

<u>*Chapter 6*</u>

Over
The
Edge

I do remember the first time I witnessed my sister drugged up.

My mom was coming down the street and she was telling me she did not know where my sister was at, but thought she could be in this house around the corner.

Without hesitation, I ran to that house. When I reached the house, I asked for my sister.

There were four men there who stood looking nervous. I pushed myself through and ran up the duplex steps to find another man splashing water on my sister's completely naked body in the tub.

She was completely out of it. Her eyes were closed, her neck was not supporting her head and her body was in the tub lifeless.

Immediately, I became so angry that I punched the man in the face, then grabbed him by his neck and forced him into the living room.

I just continued to punch him several times. Two of the men tried to restrain me to keep me from punching the man while one of them stood by the door and watched.

I punched one of the men that tried to restrain me in the face, and rushed the other one, pushing him through a window. I was so upset, frustrated and hurt that all I could do is cry while all of this was going on.

I believe the tears and anger fueled my strength and intensity. With my eyes full of tears, and my body full of rage, I remember going back to the bathroom and took off my shirt, put it on my sister and carried her home.

While this entire ordeal was occurring, my mother was back at our house. I remember carrying my sister home and leaving her with my mom.

Later that night, when I returned home, my sister had sobered up and I took it upon myself to tell her how I felt.

I started to yell and scream at her, calling her names. I remember saying, "You're nasty! Disgusting! Ugh!"

I also recall asking her, "Do you even care what people think about you?"

I told her everything I wanted to say in all the wrong ways. I was yelling and screaming at my sister like I was her father, not her brother.

She was not receptive to any of it because of my approach.

Who would have ever known that night would be the last time I saw my sister?

This situation crushed my soul.

If you see someone you love for the last time, you do not want to tell them how disgusted you are with them; you want to tell them how much you love them and how much you care for them.

Regardless of the situation, you want your last words to be your true feelings, and I felt like my last encounter with my sister was the total opposite.

In my heart, I felt I knew who was responsible for my sister's struggle with drugs and I was not going to let him ruin my family any longer.

My mom's boyfriend had destroyed what was left of my family.

I decided to steal a gun from my great aunt's house.

My little cousin who was about 10 years younger than me, had previously showed me a gun stored in my great aunt's house.

Our great aunt was elderly, and my little cousin said he was scared she would do something she shouldn't do with the gun.

I knew she stored the gun in a guest bedroom, and I had made the decision that I was going to take it.

I took the .38 special and assured my little cousin I was taking it so she would not hurt herself or anybody else just to keep him quiet.

But, I also had another alternative in mind; my mom's boyfriend had impacted my family one too many times and I was going to protect my family.

I was going to stop my mom's boyfriend.

My day came, he was not going to hurt my family anymore; I remember it like it was yesterday. My mom's boyfriend and she had gotten in to fight and I knew I was not going to allow him to hurt anyone else in my family again.

Plus, I felt he was responsible for my sister's disappearance and I had no clue if she was dead or alive.

So, I rushed up the stairs grabbed the gun from my room and pointed it right in his face.

He grabbed an iron and clocked me in the face. My mom called the police, I dropped the gun and ran to meet with my mentor from a court ordered program.

My mentor called my mom, and they both agreed that it would be best for me to stay with him for a while.

For quite some time, I was upset with my mom because I could not believe she would call the police on me when I was only trying to protect her.

Now I know it was God's intervention, because if I would have continued with my plan that day, I know I would not be in the position I am in today.

My mom and her boyfriend eventually went to prison after my sister was found in Arkansas in a prostitution ring.

My sister was arrested as an adult, sent to jail under a stolen identity and happened to write a letter to my Nana that overturned everything.

My Nana gave the letter to my sister's probation officer, and eventually, the case ended up in federal court.

The state of Ohio was trying to convince Arkansas that the little girl in jail that they booked as a woman, actually was a minor.

It also made front page of a local newspaper and was a hot topic on TV stations.

When my mom went to prison, she said it was our fault.

Those comments hurt us, and everyone I shared my deepest feelings with said I had the right to be offended.

But God said, no!

At this point, me and my sister already had moved out of our house and were staying with mentors from the court ordered programs we were in, along with the approval of my mom and them.

CSB (Children Services Board) tried to come take us back into custody, but our mentors worked hard to receive their foster care license to keep us.

My mom spent many years in prison. She and her boyfriend were convicted of prostituting my sister, her daughter.

Chapter 7

All My Life
I
Had To Fight

Growing up, fighting was my outlet.

I could not even tell you how many fists fights I was involved in. Although there were too many to count, I must admit, I did lose a few.

Here are some of the stories.

I remember fighting as early as first-grade in Catholic school while living with my Nana.

There was one kid I would repeatedly fight and break his glasses every time I punched him in the face.

My grandmother had to pay to get him new glasses three times.

We fought over the stupid stuff.

If he disagreed with me, I would punch him if the face. If he yelled at me, I would punch him in the face. If he liked the girl I liked I would punch him. My limited social skills were communicated through my behavior.

While placed at Big Momma house, I was in three fights in the same day on my first day of school.

I walked to school with my new foster brother, who happened to be in the same grade, but a different class.

As we were walking to school, we met up with other kids on the way.

Some of the kids kept referencing me as, "New Boy," and I continued to correct them by telling them, " My name is Deonte."

One kid got upset and told me not to get smart.

And right in front of the school, we duked it out, right there.

I got the best of him and earned a little respect that morning from some of my peers.

However, the cousins of the kid I beat up had it out for me the minute I walked in the school.

I was taken into the office because of the fight.

While I sat there and waited on the principal, one of the cousins of one of the kids I fought that morning met me in the office.

He asked if he could talk to me in the hall while I waited for the principal.

And another fight ensued right outside the principal's office.

The school told Big Momma she had to come to the school, and the principal did not suspend me after I explained what happen.

She was willing to let me finally meet my teacher, on my first day, at my new school.

As soon as I got to the classroom, it was time to go to lunch.

I was confronted by another student about fighting his two cousins.

I took it upon myself to not back down from the kid as he punched me in my face.

I stood there as if to prove to the kid that that his punch did not hurt or affect me as the teacher ran to break up the fight.

As I stood realizing I had just been in my third fight of the day and was punched in the face and did not retaliate, I burst into tears.

I was sent to office again, and Big Momma had to come back to take me home.

Unfortunately, this was only the beginning of a life full of fist fights.

I fought every day in junior high and high school, and I used my home life as an excuse to express my frustrations using violence.

Most of the drug dealers in my neighborhood were kids who went to my school.

These kids would try to tease me about what my mom or sister did for money or drugs.

Growing up back then, I could talk about my family, but no one else could, or it would be a problem.

This mindset always lead to an altercation. During this time in my life, I felt like everybody was against me, and the school system never saw things in my favor.

I would come to school one day and a student would talk about my family, so he and I would get into a fight.

No sooner than when I come back from suspension, another student would have something else to say about my family, so I would get into another fight.

Once I return from that suspension, another student would disrespect my family, so again, I would get suspended for defending my family.

Time and time again, this would occur.

Due to me always fighting, the school system labeled me as the problem child. The administration would look at the situation, seeing that each of those students have been in one fight, and I would have been involved in multiple fights.

I was quickly labeled as the instigator by me being in numerous fights which resulted in them suspending or expelling me.

I remember my first time getting jumped.

What a day!

I was on my way to a court ordered Anger Management Class when I was jumped by some kids who went to my school.

I was required to complete this course as part of the terms for my probation, and I use to ride my bike to the class.

Sometimes, I would stop at the park before class, then ride my bike downtown to attend the court ordered sessions.

On this day, I was jumped by two students who left me with a bloody nose and busted lip.

I still managed to make my way to class and showed up with a leaking nose and busted lip.

I assume the counselors felt bad for me because they said I didn't have to attend any more session if I had to travel through those circumstances.

Another time I was jumped after attending a party that girls from my school hosted.

I was invited to go to this party by some of the girls in my school, and I really wanted to go because I really liked one of them.

The girls gassed me up, talking about, "You're so funny! You have to come!"

I was hesitant because I had just beat up one of the girl's boyfriend pretty bad a week earlier in school, and the party was in their neighborhood.

I asked a couple of friends if they would attend with me just in case something popped off, but due to the

party being on a school night, none of my friends'
parents would not allow them to go.

I didn't have rules or supervision at my house, so I
could do as I pleased.

The week prior to the party, I was suspended for
fighting, so I spent my days working.

My job would allow me to work when I was
suspended from school.

After working all the extra hours, I brought me a
new fresh pair of Jordan's and rode my bike to the
party myself.

As soon as I got there, it seemed like the girls were
excited to see me. They were happy, dancing and
we started to have a really good time.

When I first arrived, there were more girls than
boys.

However, in less than an hour, it seemed to be way
more boys in the party; one of whom was the boy I
had just beat up last week.

He began mean-mugging me, and of course, I stared
backed to let him know "you don't want this, you
know what just happened."

Wrong move!

What I didn't know was that he was there with his block, and they stalked me the entire time.

As I was trying to dance, all his friends would bump me and try to provoke me to fight them.

They did everything they could to start something. I just kept on dancing to the slow music until they switched it up.

As soon as they changed the music, I quickly disappeared down the steps to get on my bike to go home.

As I was running down the steps I heard, "He's trying to leave!"

I quicken my pace and ran to the side of the house to get my bike that I custom made.

As soon as I started to pedal, the chained slipped.

I looked up and I was surrounded by the entire party trying to get me to rematch the kid I had just previously beaten up.

We squared up, but I knew as soon as I threw a punch, they were going to jump me.

Because of my hesitation, he decided to try to takeoff on me.

But as soon as he threw his first punch, I pushed him to the ground and they all attacked me.

Pushed

The fight was broke up by one of our mutual friends and I was told to just get up and walk away.

As I started to walk, I noticed that I had come out of my brand-new Jordan's I purchased the day before.

I could not let it go, so I turned around and went back to get my Jordan's and my bike.

Wrong move number two!

They chased me for three blocks. I hopped in a random pickup truck and closed the door.

The owner of the truck stared at me and asked if I was okay and tried to make sense of the situation.

I am sure he was stunned that I had frantically jumped in his vehicle.

He quickly turned around to see the mob that was chasing me. He raised his hands to tell them to stop and they began punching and kicking him. I locked the doors of the truck.

After the mob passed and I unlocked the doors, the owner got back in his truck to give me a ride home.

I wanted him to drop me off and keep going. I planned on getting in my house through a window, because we always kept the front and back doors locked.

I didn't want him to see how I got in my house, but, he wanted to talk with my parents about what had just taken place.

He waited and knocked on the door, but of course, there was no answer. He waited and waited and knocked some more.

Eventually, my mom answered the door high and naked as the man tried to explain what just happen.

Before he could finish explaining the situation, my mom cut him off and said "Thanks" while slamming the door in his face.

Chapter 8

When Class-Clowning Goes Wrong

Class clowning became my defense mechanism.

I knew making my peers laugh would keep them off me, so I thought.

One time I was making fun of a student who was a transfer from St. Louis.

He decided to share with the class that he was senior in our freshmen class.

What made him do that?

I made fun of this kid the entire class period.

I mean joke, after joke, after joke until he became visually upset.

Even then, I followed him to his bus still cracking jokes.

Once we reached the bus line up, I realized he rode the same bus as me, so the joke continued.

I went from talking about his mama, to his hair, and even the way he looked. The jokes kept coming.

At some point during this crack session, I began referencing this kid as St. Louis. He eventually got so upset that he cussed at me on the bus.

Everyone on the bus thought this was so funny, so I decided to take things up a notch and told St. Louis he would pay for cussing at me as soon as he got off the bus.

He appeared unalarmed, so I made sure to let him know that we were going to fight due to him cussing at me.

The bus stopped and St. Louis got off the bus so quickly I thought he was attempting to run.

After being hyped up by other students, I was in high pursuit and gave him chase only to end up in a trap.

As I chased him off the bus, I decided to jump in the air to avoid the steps to continue chasing St. Louis, who unfortunately had not continued running but was waiting with a ready punch for my face.

He hit me dead in my face while I was still in midair. I felt so much power, velocity and anger in that punch as I fell to the snow.

By the time I hit the ground, St. Louis had already grabbed me and began wrestling with me for a while in the snow. The entire school bus watched me in disbelief as the bus finally pulled off.

The next day at school, everyone was talking about how the new kid beat up Deonte, and everybody was asking when I planned to fight him again.

Feeling like failing to fight a second time was not an option; my pride took off and I hyped up the class that St. Louis and I were in together.

I told everybody I was going to fight him again in class.

Everybody except me was hype.

The truth was that I did not want to see St. Louis fist hit my face again.

I knew the power he possessed in those hands. So, I quickly developed a plan.

I mentally decided I was going to fight him in front of the teacher.

In my mind, I knew no teacher would just allow us to fight for very long, so I would have just enough time to get a couple good hits in before the fight would come to a halt.

Everyone knew the fight was scheduled to happen and rushed to class on time and ready, except the teacher.

As the bell rung, the teacher stated she needed to leave the class to make copies for the day's lesson, which left me completely shook up.

My well thought out plan was not developing with the teacher leaving the class unattended in mind.

I knew the only thing I could do was hype myself up to do what I felt at that time was the inevitable.

When the teacher exited, I immediately started throwing chairs and desk to hype myself up and hopefully scare St. Louis.

Unfortunately for me, that plan didn't work. St. Louis did not appear scared at all, but he did tell me he did not want to fight only because he did not want to risk getting suspended.

No sooner than he released those words from his mouth, I took the opportunity lunge at St. Louis to hit him before he hit me with that same anger and velocity he used the day prior.

I punched him so hard out of fear, and immediately put him in a headlock with this same adrenaline to avoid getting hit again.

I remember hoping so strongly that I could hold on long enough for an adult to walk in the room as he tried to get away.

While I had a death grip on him and felt like I was fighting for my life as he struggled to get out of the hold, I remember repeatedly punching him just to keep him from getting free from my hold.

At that point, I don't even remember punching him to do harm or win the fight; I just knew if I slipped up and let him out of that hold, it would be over for me.

After what felt like a lifetime, the hall monitors came to the class, broke up the fight, and sent us to the office. We were both suspended for 10 days. I just knew that everyone was going to becoming up to me after school on the bus ride home to tease me because they seen the fear on my face. To my surprise student did rush me, but everyone was talking about hearing about me beating up St. Louis.

Unfortunately, St. Louis had no fear. They next day St. Louis showed up to my house which happened to be down the street from his house. He wanted to confront me and have a third fight. After looking out my window, I realized it was best to act as if I was not at home. Two days later days later I received notice that St. Louis was no longer living on our block and he had moved back to St. Louis. I hide in the house for two days.

What I learned from this situation was you have to treat people the way you want to be treated.

Picking a fight with St. Louis and calling him names related to what I experienced at Big Mommas' house my first day of school, when I was new, and the kids called me "New Boy."

Victims sometimes become the offender as a result of being victimized. St. Louis set me straight quick.

Class clowning back fired on me a couple times.

I remember my first day of kindergarten class and the teacher said it was nap time. I told her I was not tired and I did not want to take a nap and stood on my cot refusing to lay down.

She told me I could just stand there if I was quiet.

I guess standing while all the other kids were sleeping became boring, because at some point, I fell asleep.

When I finally woke up, all the kids were coming back in from recess that I missed due to my late nap. I never refused nap time ever again.

In second grade, I had a teacher who I know quit her job because of my behavior. I gave her pure hell.

One time I cried so badly in class because I received an "F" in a subject.

The teacher agreed to change my grade if I promised to be better in class and school.

I agreed, got home and still received a whooping for the "C" I had earned which originally was an "F."

I exhibited crazy behavior the next day in school and my teacher quit. I never saw that teacher again.

Chapter 9

Decisions
Without
Guidance

Pushed

The first time I was arrested, I was in the third-grade.

I took a knife to my Catholic school.

I don't know why I did, I just know I spent the entire day at the juvenile detention center.

I was only 7 years old, and unfortunately, the story was published in the local newspaper.

The second time I was arrested was the result of me class clowning again and struggling to accept that I was on the receiving end of the joke.

I was at a different school and a student made a joke on me that left me upset.

I could not wait to see him at lunch so that I could punch him in his face.

As I attempted to run up to him in the lunchroom, the gym teacher and two other teachers tried to hold me back.

During the struggle, one of the teachers claimed I assaulted him.

Consequently, I was charged with three counts of assault and placed on probation at such an early age.

I had the same probation officer every time I was on probation.

He understood what I was going through and would give me advice to help to get me through system.

Eventually, I got off probation and got into SBH (Severe Behavior Handicap) Classes and eventually the name was changed to ED (Emotionally Disturbed) Classes.

After being oversexualized, I lost my virginity at the age of 12, not to long before my sexual assault I endured took place.

When I was 15 years old, I planned a pregnancy with my girlfriend.

I wanted to be loved by someone and I felt having a child would create a love I was missing and searching for. I wanted to start a family and vowed that I would create an atmosphere where love was real, and family would never leave or abandon each other.

My girlfriend at the time made me feel better and she acted like she cared; she thought I was funny.

I knew I could be entering foster care soon again because of my home situation. So we planned on having the baby so we would be able to stay close.

Plus I did not want her to be taken away from me being that I felt she loved me, Well she told me she loved me.

At this point in my life, I did what I wanted to do. I had no voices in my ear telling me what was right and what was wrong.

I was just trying to figure out what I was going through and what made it better at the moment was someone telling me they loved and cared for me.

It made me feel better. So, I made decisions that could have waited.

I had my first daughter at age 14 going on 15 and planned it. A decision I believe I should of waited to make until I was a married adult. The crazy part is that I am truly proud and blessed to have 2 beautiful daughters now and I could never picture life without them.

<u>*Chapter 10*</u>

Convicted
By My
Perception

I was molested at a very young age by a female member of my family.

She performed oral sex on me as a kid. I was exposed to sexual activity at an early age.

My sisters and me would sneak into my mother and boyfriend's bedroom where the kept all kinds of pornographic material.

We would sneak and watch the DVDs.

I was sexual assaulted by a neighbor who stayed on his porch drinking and smoking everyday day after he came home from prison.

He would buy all the kids ice cream from the ice cream truck and even give us food stamps to go to the corner store to buy us bags of chips and different snacks.

He groomed me by the money and gifts and even would let me drink with him when I was around 11 or 12 years old.

One time he invited me upstairs from his porch to his apartment and he proceeded to let me drink until I was unconscious or unresponsive.

I just needed to lay there for a while because the alcohol had taken its effect.

He attempted to pull my pants off. I got upset and tried to get up and leave telling him I was not like that.

He responded that I could not leave. He had a look in his eyes as though he was not going back to jail.

And if I tried to leave, there would be a fight. I was scared, he then assaulted me. I was too embarrassed to mention and even tell anyone.

This led me to the point of having a great homophobia and hating any man who considered himself a homosexual.

I had five uncles on my mom's side of the family. The oldest uncle I had around the time of my assault, just recently passed away from a drug overdose.

I had two other uncles who I loved and would visit - especially my uncle James - who were two heterosexual males who kept me laughing and would always seem to keep me smiling through some the hardest times in my life.

I had identical twin set of twin uncles, one was gay and performed in adult movies and one was bisexual and was in the army.

Around the same time, both uncles contracted the HIV virus, which eventually turned to AIDS.

One of my twin uncles who became sick with AIDS, eventually moved in with us and was on his death bed.

I resented and disliked him for his open flamboyant gay lifestyle.

We would regularly argue and even got in to a fist fight at one point in time before they both eventually passed away from the Aids virus.

I would not be convicted of my homophobia or hate for who practices gay or bisexual lifestyles until years later.

As a young adult while at a bible study, I did not really want to participate because there were who I believed were very feminine, flamboyant gay men. The time came to pray, and I was refusing in my mind to not to hold any of their hands in prayer because I felt I really disliked gay men because of my sexual assault.

That's when one of those men told a testimony very similar to mine about him being molested.

And an instant conviction hit me. I asked myself, who do I think I am or better than because of the way it affected him was different than my experience?

I still do believe whole heartedly a man should be with a woman and a woman should be with a man.

I still also understand how an assault or molestation can effect a person differently, although very different from my experience.

I know and believe that God created and intended for man to be with woman and woman to be with man. I believe the only way a person can get to their truths is building their relationship with God and that I believe goes for anything unlike God.

Chapter 11

Sister! Sister!

Although my sisters brought me many troubles growing up, I couldn't imagine life without them.

I remember when my maternal grandmother caught them trying to smoke cigarettes and decided she would use it as a teaching moment for all of us.

She told us that if we wanted to smoke, we had to pass a test and that we could smoke whenever we wanted.

I never had an urge to smoke, but I welcomed the challenge. I knew kids weren't supposed to smoke or even know how to smoke, so the opportunity sparked an interest trying to pass what she called, "The Test."

My grandmother brought us all a pack of cigarettes and a pack of chewing tobacco. She made us smoke a pack each and chew the bag of chewing tobacco and swallow the juice. I was sick for what felt like three months, and I never wanted to smoke anything again.

My baby sisters got me caught up in in a lot of situations.

One of them would always get me into trouble and fights. She wasn't a very good fighter, but was very bossy and attitudinal.

She once got into a fist fight with her younger childhood friend. Unbeknownst to my sister, she got beat up.

This little girl really got up, dust herself off and told the girl if she kept talking she was going get it again.

My sister's confidence and approach even had the other little girl confused, because afterward, she agreed my sister had won the fight.

I remember one time my sister was scared the popular kids at her school were going to beat her up because they were making fun of her.

My other sister came to her aid and got jumped by the classmates. She was left bloody while the same sister who initially was involved in the drama, ran home.

The outcome surprised me, because I've seen my sister get jumped on numerous occasions, and still take turns beating up the culprits.

She wasn't innocent by far and was well known for her ability to scuffle. I am not sure how she ended up on the defeated end of this fight, but I ran up to the school to confront the individuals.

The following day, they all came to the park to fight me with my little sister who had now become their friend.

I couldn't believe my eyes. As a child, my little sister was something unexplainable.

When we would argue as kids, she always knew what buttons to press.

One of the things I hated most when growing up was my bad acne. My sister knew I was so embarrassed about my acne.

Every time we got into an argument, she would call me a bumpy face b****.

I hated it. We even got into a fist fight and a throwing match one day after name calling.

The police were called. Upon their arrival, they immediately snatched me up. This same little sister came to my aid to stop them from harming me.

I guess her calling me a bumpy faced b**** didn't mean she hated my guts after all.

Those bumps gave me the blues.

I remember being in music class and being told to line up one afternoon. We would always race to the door to get ready to go to our next class, and everyone wanted to get there first.

On this particular day, I won and turned around to see a female student who was upset about not being first. She looked me dead in my face and said, "It's about to burst," referring to the bumps on my face. I was so embarrassed.

<u>*Chapter 12*</u>

Opportunities
Are Everywhere,
I Love My Mama!

I learned to take advantage of every opportunity at a very young age. I get it naturally. My mom has always been an opportunist, or hustler. She would bamboozle any system or religion if they were offering help. As a kid, we practiced so many religions. My family joined any religion offering help to families. I have been Catholic, Mormon, Jehovah Witness, and every other religion under the sun. If they bought us a couch or put groceries in our house, we would join to reap the benefits.

The extent to her creative approaches to optimizing opportunities exceeded beyond religious practices. One day, after coming from bible study with one of the many churches we joined, I was excited to hear a fire truck nearby. I jumped out of the church van and ran in the street to look for the fire truck. To my surprise, the sirens were a lot closer than I thought. The fire truck pushed it breaks as hard as it could and still managed to smack me. I flew in the air and was in the air so long that I had time to think about how I wanted to position myself for the landing. I ended up landing on both the curb and street. I got up quickly and ran in the house. I continued running until I was upstairs and jumped in my bed under the covers. My mom chased after me, and the fire men chased after her to check on me. My mom entered the room first and asked if I was okay. I told her I was fine. She immediately looked me in my eyes and stated, "Act like you're hurt, we are about to get paid!"

Pushed

As soon as she spoke those words the fire men entered in to the room and asked if I was alright. I replied, "Yes," and my mom gave me the dirtiest look I have ever seen. I immediately knew that look meant for me to rethink my reply and act as if my leg had been broken. I quickly recanted my initial statement, and they called an ambulance. My mom refused ride in the ambulance due to the cost attached to being transported in an ambulance. The church van dropped us off at the emergency room, and we waited to be seen.

As we entered the back room, the nurses came in and out of the room periodically. With every exit, my mom ransacked another drawer in the room and stole everything she could get her hands on. The nurse came back in looking for stuff that was gone and notice my mom had stuffed bandages in her bra. The nurse was bold and asked for them back. My mom put up an argument saying she needed the items for home. The nursed told her she needed to return the items, or the police would be called.

My mom gave some items back and the doctor came in to check me out. Of course, I was fine, but with every glare from my mom, I played hurt. The doctor released me and stated I had sprained my knee.

On the way out, my mom attempted to steal an oxygen tank and we were chased by police. While I am still in a newly placed brace, we ran to the parking lot where my mom ditched the tank and ran to the bus stop to catch the bus. As an adult, I got the courage to ask her, "Mom, why did you try to steal that oxygen tank?"

She replied, "I needed to breathe!" All I could do at that time was laugh, and say, "I love my Mama!".

Gifts from my mom were rare, so when she told me had bought me some new Nike tennis shoes from a garage sale for like 5 dollars I beyond excited. She would not let me wear them until the first day of school. So, when that day came I was so excited for the day to finally arrive. I was so ready. I got up early and ran all the way to school in the rain. As soon as I reached my locker, I opened my book bag and threw on my new shoes. I knew I was ready for the first day, and I was about to be fresh. After lacing my shoes, tying them, and standing up to walk on the shiny newly polished hallway floors I began sliding everywhere. My shoes were making a clicking sound and very slippery because they weren't tennis shoes, but a pair of cleats.

<u>*Chapter 13*</u>

Running From My Reality

Running away for me wasn't always peaches and cream. I would often try to escape the reality caused by my mother and her crazy boyfriend. Through these episodes on the run, I gained many survival skills. Many of my days on the run included sleeping in laundry rooms until morning, and then heading to the mall during the time when senior citizens are walking in circles to get exercise.

One time I had been on the run for about a week. I decided to visit my Nana, and she gave me some money. After leaving her house I continued with my routine and went to kill some time at the mall. I always knew I could get something to eat at the mall because of this lady that would give me free pretzels from the pretzel shop. It was as if she knew I was on the run, and felt the need to keep me fed.

One day while I was at the pretzel shop, these three beautiful girls came up and started teasing each other stating, "Ugh, look at your boyfriend" referencing me. I was filthy and dirty and had been wearing the same clothes every day. They were all in denial and blaming each other. After immediately trying to combat the hurt I just felt by from their comments, I looked and pulled my money that I received from my grandmother stating, "I got money though!" The beautiful girl in the middle replied, "He do got money," and shortly after told me she would be my girlfriend.

This little girl did not even know my name and continued to call me every name in the book, except Deonte as she escorted me through every store in the mall just, so I could spend the entire $100 dollars I had on her. After I was broke, I walked back to my neighborhood to sleep in a meat shed near my house.

I spent many nights in that shed, however, when it was cold outside, I got creative. I would seek out warmer places to sleep. One day while it was snowing and freezing temperatures, I decided to walk to an apartment complex where I knew of a classmate who let me spend the night. The following day their parent asked to speak with my parents, and immediately knew something was up when I refused and asked to spend the night again. She called the police and I jumped off the balcony and lead the police on a foot chase. Initially, I lost them, however, I got tired and gave up running. They caught me and took me back to my parent's home.

Chapter 14

Academics

Now I have been in a lot of schools. I believe I have been blessed to be versatile because that reason. I have been to Catholic schools, Behavior schools, public schools, and suburban schools. One time in high school I almost received straight A's when I lived with a foster parent, but the music teacher gave me a "C" in music I was devastated.

I know I was a hand full and very challenging for teachers. By the 6th grade I was placed on an Individualized Education Plan (IEP) and assigned to SBH (Severe Behavior Handicap) classes primarily due to my inability to display appropriate behavior. Reflecting, I realize I did so much to teachers while I was in school. I recall jumping through a teacher window just to scare her and the class while she was teaching.

On another occasion, I was able to recognize my teacher was growing tired of my disruptive behaviors and was ready to send me out of the classroom. In the sincerest voice I could simulate, I asked, "Why are you always kicking me out of class?" As the teacher attempted to explain, I would stand up, cut him off like my favorite wrestler at the time (THE ROCK), and scream in the middle of the class, "It doesn't matter why you're kicking me out." Although the class thought this was hilarious, this decision costed me a 5-day suspension.

I wish I could say that was the last time I was disruptive and disrespectful to an adult. Unfortunately, I thought I was above the rules and thought I could do what I want, when I want, anywhere I wanted. This unrealistic theory was snatched out of me really quick by a football coach one day.

I recall being in 9th grade walking the hallways when I should have been in class. The football coach was monitoring the halls, and he asked me, "Where are you supposed to be?' I replied, "Quit F***ing talking to me" and continued walking toward the restroom. As I walked into the bathroom and entered a stall to pee, he kicked the door opened and grabbed me my by my neck and shirt as I urinated all down my pants. He told me if I ever talked to him that way again he would put me in my place. He pushed me down in the stall and he walked out. I grabbed my urine filled pants and ran to the office to inform the administration what had just transpired. They called the football coach in to the office asked if he had done it, he declined, and they sent me back to class. As an adult, I ran into this football coach and thanked him.

<u>*Chapter 15*</u>

Son!
Teach Me…

I could probably count how many times I had seen my father before the age of 21. One time as I kid I ran into my father at a corner store and he had no idea who I was. I died inside that day because I could not believe that the man who made me did not recognize me. I wouldn't see my father until years later when I was visiting my Grandmother and my father happen to be there. I felt the only reason my father acknowledged or recognize me because of my grandmother's excitement. He called me son and tried to hug me, but I was upset. I told him he was not my dad and he got really upset. But so was I, he yelled and scream and told me I was not going to disrespect him in his mother's house. As he screaming spit was just flying all over my face. I told him to stop spitting in my face he told me he brought me in to this world and he would take me out and continued to spit. I punched my dad in the face. My father fell back in amazement and quickly hopped up to his feet to choke the life out of me. I felt like my father held my neck until I was about a second from life. My nana screaming get off him you're going to kill him stop, while hitting him with a sturdy napkin.

I would not see my father again until I was an adult ironically at a corner store I had just got back from Europe working with kids who parents were fighting in the war in Iraq. When I pulled up to the store and noticed my father standing outside of it that I had not seen for years. I did not know what would happen. I know last altercation I had with my father resulted in a fist fight. As I left my vehicle and entered the corner store I did not know what to expect. I got what I needed from the store and walked out to come face to face with my father who looked me dead in my eye and just busted out in to tears and started reciting everything he knew and heard about me and my sisters to my surprise. He begged me to contact him to talk to him. He apologized for being absent in my life we exchanged numbers and I followed up by inviting him to my church I attended every week. One Sunday I had a conversation with my father that changed my life after one Sunday attending church. We left church service where the spirit had really moved, and my father got into the car an asked me to teach him how to become a man? I was shocked and could not comprehend what the man who made me. My biological father was saying. But he continued and said teach me how to become a man? All my life I had issues I did not know how to deal with that's why I sold drugs and use drugs and was in out prison. But you son had many issues to growing up and, in your life, but you faced them head on and became successful through them. He said that's a real man. From that moment on I looked at my life totally different I use to think I could not wait to be successful in my life, so I could make my parents wish they were a part of my life and wish they would have been there to take part in my successes but god was showing that my job and my journey was to go through what I had to endure to go back and get my family so generational curses could be broken. God was preparing me to become the Joseph of my family and the Moses of my generation.

Chapter 16

Forgiving

My

Mom

Oprah said, "Forgiveness is giving up the hope that things could have been different." Iyana fix your life said," Forgiveness is not for the perpetrator but the victim to move on." Initially, I did not understand how my mother could sell her body, or even teach my sister to sell her body too. However, one day I was able to sit down with my mom in a one on one supervised setting with my behavior coach, and asked her, "Why?" My mom who had been abandon and grew up in an orphanage replied, "I am Hoe! I have always been a hoe, and I am going to continue to be a Hoe." That day my mom went in to detail how her biological father (who was with her mother only when he was away from his main family) would molest and prostitute her to his friends at a very young age. That day I looked at my mom situation different. I saw my mother through a fresh set of eyes. I understood more about how she processed things. I no longer looked at her as just an awful parent, she was conditioned. I never condoned her actions, but now I understood.

Years later God would bring to my attention the need for me to forgive my mom. My mom would reach out from prison, but none of us would talk to her. We felt she was bogus for blaming us for her going to prison. But God brought to my attention that my mom who was a drug addict was not thinking clearly before she left for prison. She made decisions under the influence of drugs. As she set in prison thinking in her sober mind all the wrong she committed, she was attempting to fix things by reach out to us and trying to make amends. She was trying to fix her wrongs and we were pushing her away. God spoke to me and said, "Forgive her." When someone is wrong they know they are wrong. When a person reaches out to make amends, and you push them away they are more likely to go back to what numb them before. In my mom case, her numbing agent was drugs, money, and men. God told me to forgive my mom and we believe because we chose to follow God's lead, my mom has been clean for years.

Chapter 17

The Power
Of
Caring Adults

Through all this I realized the power of relationship or a caring adult. I did not know how to cope with so much I was going through until caring adults came into my life who motivated, inspired, and encouraged me not to be defined by my past but to become the greatest me I could be. I had at teacher who knew what I was going through at home and refuse to kick me out of class for class clowning and made sit in class in silence for 40 minutes of the 45-minute class. She told me I would not disrupt everyone chance to learn and that I would sit in the back and remain silent until five minutes left of class and I could have the Deonte Moss Show. What eventually happened is I remained quite in class until I got so bored I started doing my work and would even be caught missing the Deonte Moss Show due to me finishing my work I started.

I had a Mentor a father Figure who Love God with his whole heart and was charismatic and a considerable influence on my life that I wanted to be just like him, but he would always tell me that that he wanted me to be better than him. He took me into his home and loved me like his real son and I loved him for that.

I had a pastor who was there for me in every major part in my life in becoming a man, in myself and Marriage who molded me and gave me advise to becoming who I am today. I had a probation officer, a boss, a judge who gave me second chances and did not want to see me fail. A uncle who made me smile or laugh every time he was in my presence these relationship were detrimental in the process of me becoming the Greatest Deonte Moss I could be and I would not be who I am if it was not for the push of these caring adults who reminded me of

Chapter 18

From
Behavior Kid
To
Behavior Coach

I remember the first time I met My Behavior Coach he came to my house for a home visit when I was court ordered to enter a program where he was employed. He met my Mom and introduced himself to me. What I remember most about that day was my Behavior Coach asking my mom how I was doing and what she felt I was going through. My mother answered and said that she had no clue and did not know why I choose to misbehave. She stated she had tried everything to help me. I was so upset because I felt my mom was not being truthful. I felt like she had nothing to do with me and was consumed in her crack addiction and prostitution. I was so mad that she would act like she tried to help me when she wouldn't even be home or disappeared for months at a time. I remember being so furious that I raised my voice and called my Mom a liar. My Behavior Coach then asked if he could have a second with me. He took me to the porch and told me to my face, "Don't you ever disrespect your mother again in my presence, you only get one mother," and he reminded me that she was mine.

For the past 15 years I have dedicated my life to advocating for Youth and community as mentor or in atmospheres who were able to help me build between families and communities to be able to tell my story. I have work in schools, after school programs, YMCA, united ways, boys and girls clubs, boy's scouts, youth and family programs the list goes on and on. I have created an facilitated programs with colleagues such Push program to help reduce suspension and acts of violence in a school setting while working with parent teachers, students and administrator. Press play an after-school program dedicated to creating fun atmospheres for parents, teachers, and students. Oath Program (Overcoming Adversity Through Humility) where we go motivate and encourage and inspire youth who are incarcerated. Life (Leading Individuals through the Foster care Experience) motivational speaking to kids who are in foster care.

Moss enterprises creating jobs for kids who are incarcerated so they don't have to go back to their old lifestyles.

Act (Ambitious Children's Theatre) preforming in schools and communities.

Kids (Kids Inspired by Dreams and Success) where kids and adults motivate each other by what they been through and had to endure. And the book to tell everyone who I am and what I been through does not define me. And although my parents made a lot of mistakes those mistakes do not define me but made who I am to give back. These programs and jobs have been therapeutic in way and a blessing being able to mold and make me who I am today.

Hurt people, hurt people and I was hurt, and felt no one loved me, no one cared. Life was not adding up and no one should want to live like this. I would pray and just wished one person could understand what was happening in my life and understand that I was hostage to a life I did not choose for me and I felt helpless.

 BUT GOD told me to Pray Until something happens every day and I did, but it wasn't until I started to grow and P>R>A>Y Every Day where he took me where he wanted me. Gave me my purpose.

Gods Plan

Jerimiah 29:11

"For I know the plans I have for you," declares the LORD, "plans to prosper you and not to harm you, plans to give you hope and a future."

Isaiah 55:8-9

"For my thoughts are not your thoughts, neither are your ways my ways, "declares the Lord.

"As the heavens are higher than the earth, so are my ways higher than your ways and my thoughts than your thoughts."

Romans 8:28

"And we know that in all things God works for the good of those who love him, who have been called according to his purpose."

Hebrews 13:8

"Jesus Christ is the same yesterday and today and forever."

Ecclesiastes 3:11

"He has made everything beautiful in its time. He has also set eternity in the human heart; yet no one can fathom what God has done from beginning to end."

Habakkuk 2:3

"For still the vision awaits its appointed time; it hastens to the end-it will not lie. If it seems slow, wait for it; it will surely come; it will not delay"

James 2:17

"In the same way, faith by itself, if it is not accompanied by action, is dead."

2 Chronicles 7:14

"If my people, which are called by my name, shall humble themselves, and pray, and seek my face, and turn from their wicked ways; then will I hear from heaven, and will forgive their sin, and will heal their land."

Psalm 51:10

"Create in me a clean heart, O God; and renew a right spirit within me."

Matthew 7:7

"Ask, and it shall be given you; seek, and ye shall find; knock, and it shall be opened unto you:"

Dedicated

To

GOD.

Thank You

Dr. Krontayia Moss

Shaniyah Moss

Nakiyah Moss

My Nana

Pam Russell

Antoine Moss

Lawrence Tribble

Shelly Slough

Daryl Q. Tucker

Dr. Pat Mckinstry

Ranisha and Desiree Moss

I Love You All......

About The Author

Deonte Moss was born in Toledo, Ohio and is familiar with many resources available to our communities. Through a challenging childhood, he gained the ability to overcome numerous obstacles and barriers with the potential to impact his quality of life. Gracefully, his past experiences have paved the way for many opportunities to encourage and motivate members of many communities.

Subsequent to graduating from high school, he attended The University of Toledo, and studied Communications and Theatre. As a result of his performance, Moss was recommended to represent the University of Toledo and granted the opportunity to travel the world while working with families on military bases in Germany. Using his engaging and charismatic personality, Deonte Moss implemented effective skill building lesson plans that promoted positive relationships, character development, and educational growth.

In 2007, He co-founded Life Institute LLC. Through Life Institute Deonte Moss served as the liaison and advocate, often bridging the lines of communication between students, parents, teachers, and the community. Life Institute has developed partnerships with Toledo Public Schools, the YMCA, and Lucas County Youth Treatment Center. Many of the programs Mr. Moss facilitated through Life Institute has been featured by several journalist and news stations.

As an advocate and community leader, Moss believes in using his life experiences to encourage, motivate, and inspire members in the communities to overcome all obstacles. Moreover, through his professional endeavors he has gained the ability to adapt in multicultural settings, and is highly motivated by the opportunity to use the knowledge gained through his educational, personal, and professional experiences. Mr. Moss communication skills, work ethics, flexibility, and his attention to detail make him a leader in his community. Moss has dedicated his life to instilling hope and He believes he possess the skills needed to be an asset to communities all over the nation.

Pushed

<u>*Notes*</u>

Deonte Moss

<u>*Notes*</u>

Pushed

<u>*Notes*</u>

Notes

Pushed

<u>Notes</u>

www.ingramcontent.com/pod-product-compliance
Lightning Source LLC
Chambersburg PA
CBHW031222090426
42740CB00007B/668